FUN with the ELECTRIC BASS

Fun with the Electric Bass is a collection of carefully arranged pieces for the electric bass. The arrangements are designed to supplement the Mel Bay Electric Bass Method.

Tuning The Electric Bass

1. Tune the 4th string in unison to the E or 19th white key to the left of middle C on the piano.
2. Place the finger behind the fifth fret of the 4th string. This will give you the tone or pitch of the 3rd string (A).
3. Place finger behind the fifth fret of the 3rd string to obtain the pitch of the 2nd string (D).
4. Place the finger behind the fifth fret of the 2nd string to obtain the pitch of the first string (G).

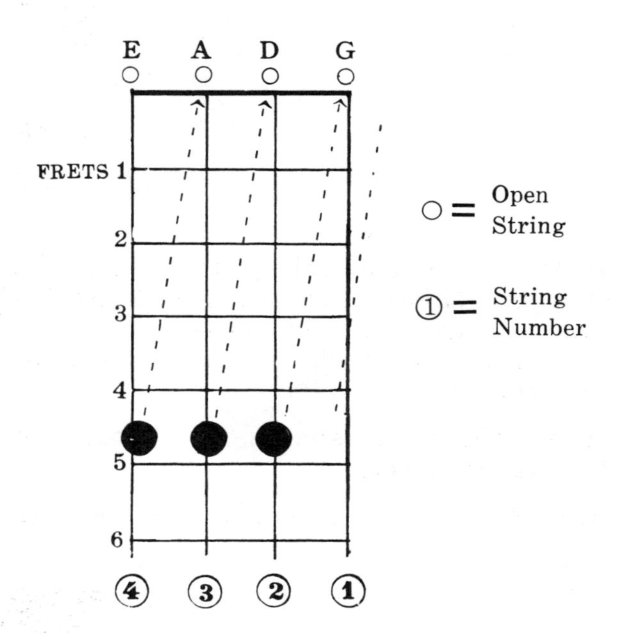

CONTENTS

1 2 3 4 5 6 7 8 9 0

Proper Playing Position

In the above illustration you will note that the first and second fingers are held relatively straight, (slightly curved) at an almost 45 degree angle in the direction of the bridge. The thumb is held under the palm of the hand, near the 4th string and pointing downward in the direction of the bridge, (in the same manner of the Jazz Bassist playing the Bass Viol with the fingers.)

When striking the strings, come to rest against the next lowest string. This method is called the Hammerstroke.

Always bear in mind to alternate the fingers whenever possible and practical.

When using a pick, pick down on quarter notes and pick down-up on eighth and sixteenth notes.

When using finger style, alternate 1st and 2nd fingers for eighth and sixteenth notes.

SYMBOLS

Number = Finger

Number Enclosed in Circle = String

Roman Numeral = Fret

GUITAR

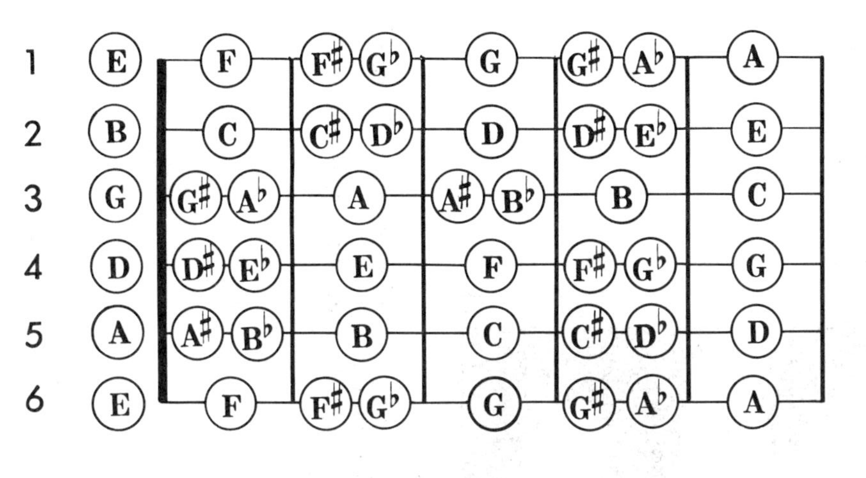

BASS GUITAR

String	Open	Fret 1	Fret 2	Fret 3	Fret 4	Fret 5
1	G	G♯ A♭	A	A♯ B♭	B	C
2	D	D♯ E♭	E	F	F♯ G♭	G
3	A	A♯ B♭	B	C	C♯ D♭	D
4	E	F	F♯ G♭	G	G♯ A♭	A

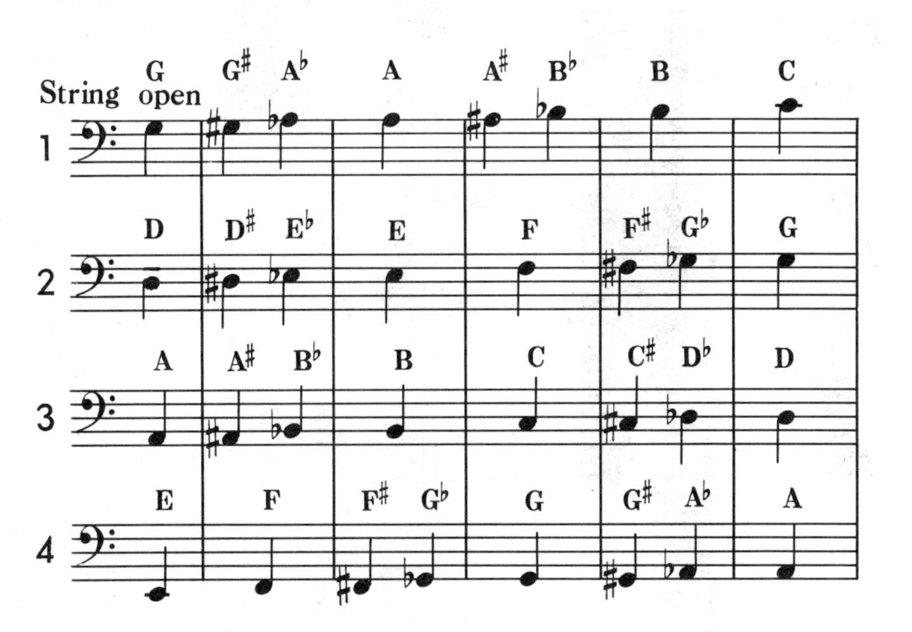

STANDARD BASS BACK GROUND

Michael, Row The Boat Ashore

3. Jordan River is chilly and cold Hallelujah!
   Chills the body but not the soul, Hallelujah!

4. Jordan River is deep and wide, Hallelujah!
   Milk and honey on the other side, Hallelujah!

5. Michael, row the boat ashore, Hallelujah!

   Michael, row the boat ashore, Hallelujah!

Number = Finger
Number Enclosed in Circle = String
Roman Number = Fret

DIXIELAND PATTERN

When The Saints Go Marching In

COUNTRY FOLK PATTERN

Lonesome Road

2. LOOK DOWN, LOOK DOWN THAT LONESOME ROAD
HANG DOWN YOUR HEAD AND CRY.
TRUE LOVE, TRUE LOVE, WHAT, HAVE I DONE?
FEEL LIKE I WANT TO DIE,

MODERN ROCK PATTERN

Rockin The Bass

See "BASS BLUES BAG" and "NEW SOUNDS FOR ELECTRIC BASS" Published By Mel Bay

The Eighth Note

An eighth note receives one-half beat. (One quarter note equals two eighth notes.) An eighth note will have a head, stem, and flag. If two or more are in successive order, they may be connected by a bar.

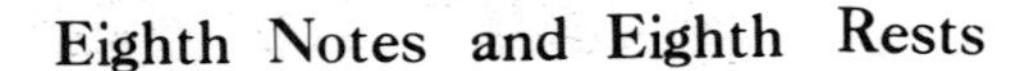

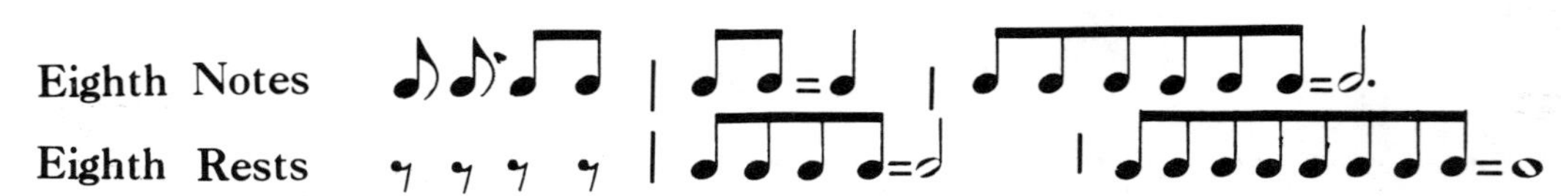

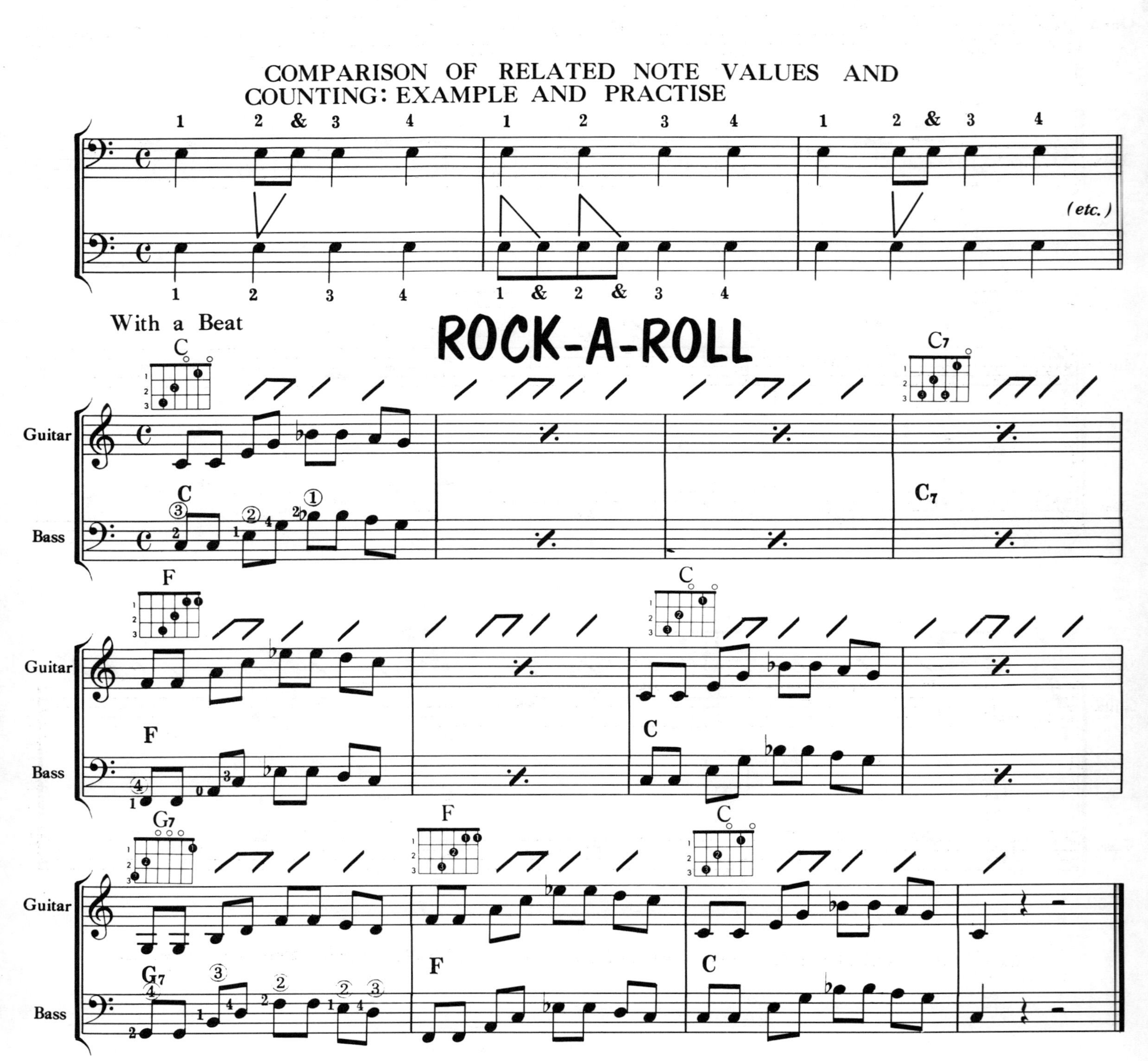

FOLK BALLAD PATTERN

Black Is The Color of My True Love's Hair

JAZZ BASS STYLE

Down By The Riverside

2. I'm gonna join hands with everyone,
   CHORUS,
3. I'm gonna put on my long white robe
   CHORUS,
4. I'm gonna talk with the Prince of Peace
   CHORUS,
5. I'm gonna bury that atom bomb
   CHORUS,

BOOGIE OR ROCK PATTERN

Boogie Woogie

BLUES WALK

Another Style Walking Pattern

(Boogie Style)

Up Tempo

TYPICAL "POP" STYLE
(Chord Progression)

Various Backup Patterns

BLUEGRASS COUNTRY STYLE

Rhody's Goose

Up Tempo

JAZZ ROCK PATTERN

WALKING JAZZ STYLE
Won't You Come Home Bill Bailey

JAZZ WALK

Traditional

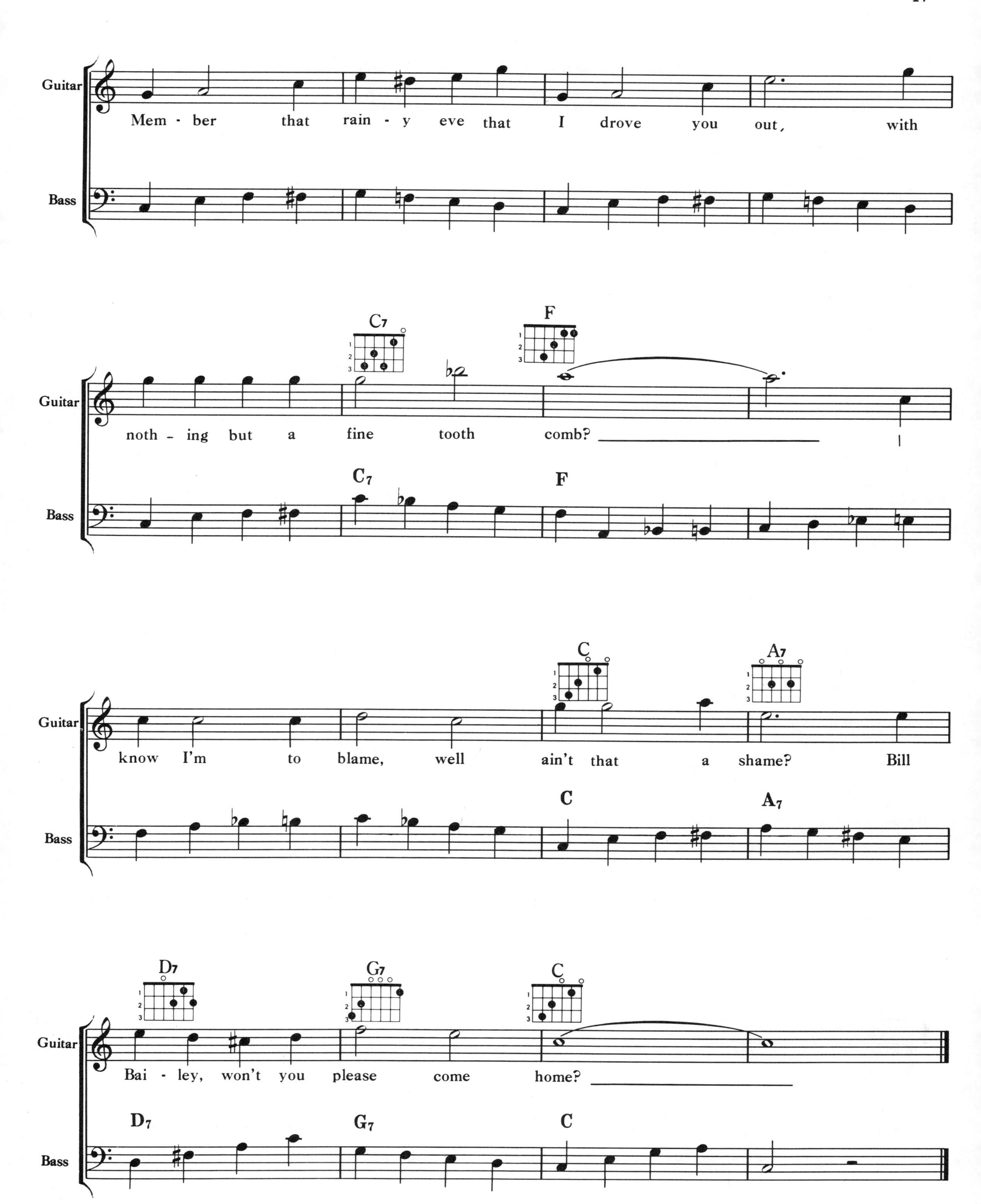
Guitar
Bass
Mem - ber that rain - y eve that I drove you out, with
C7
F
noth - ing but a fine tooth comb? I
C
A7
know I'm to blame, well ain't that a shame? Bill
D7
G7
Bai - ley, won't you please come home?

BASIC BLUES WALK

(Good For Slow Blues or fast Rock Songs)

Walking Bass Blues

For patterns like the above see "BASS BLUES BAG" – published by Mel Bay

JAZZ STYLE WALKING PATTERN

Careless Love

UP TEMPO COUNTRY JAZZ STYLE

The Wabash Cannon Ball

G C D7
Guitar
jin - gle, the rum-ble and the roar, Rid-ing through the wood-lands, to the
Bass
G C D7
hill and by the shore, Hear the might-y rush of en-gines, Hear the lone-some ho-bo's
G
squall, Rid - ing through the jun - gles on the Wa - bash Can - non - ball.
C D7 G

MOVING SACRED BACKGROUND

Just A Closer Walk With Thee

FUNKY BLUES STYLE

The Triplet

Triplets are a group of three notes played in the same time as two notes of a similar kind. Thus [triplet] would be played in the same time as [two eighth notes] or [quarter note]

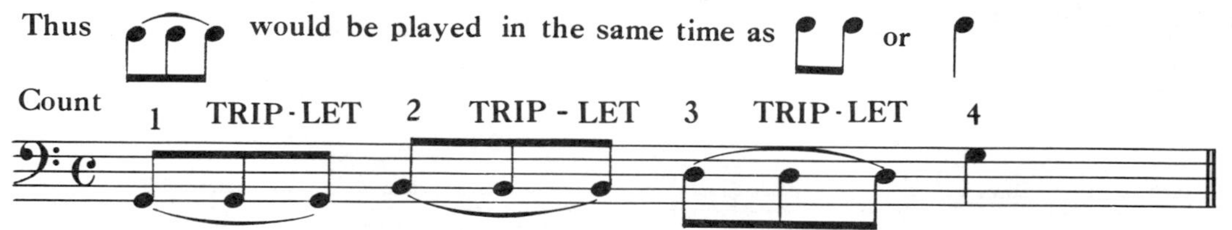

Thinking of a three syllable word can help immeasurably in getting the right division (For example: "Am-ster-dam")

Honky Tonk Blues

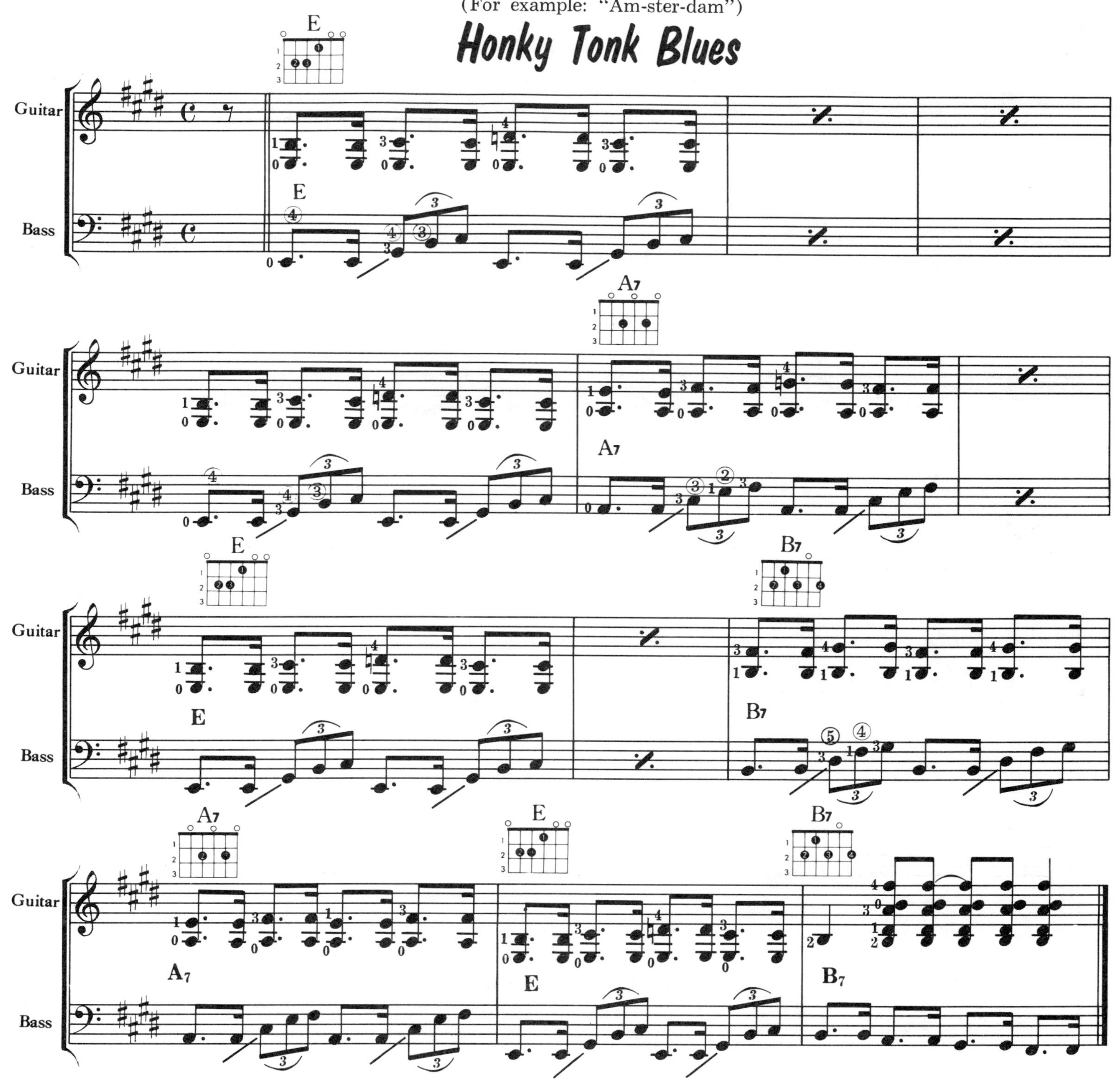

COUNTRY BLUES STYLE
F & J Blues

SOUL BASS STYLE
Hold Up

DRIVING BLUES BASS STYLE

· = CUT NOTE

WITH SHUFFLE BEAT.

12th Street And Delmar

2. Twelfth street and Delmar, you're crowdin me
Twelfth Street and Delmar, youre crowdin' me
You didn't think, that I would
Begin to see

SLOW BALLAD STYLE

FOLK BLUEGRASS STYLE

Cindy

TYPICAL GOSPEL STYLE

Amazing Grace

Slowly With Feeling

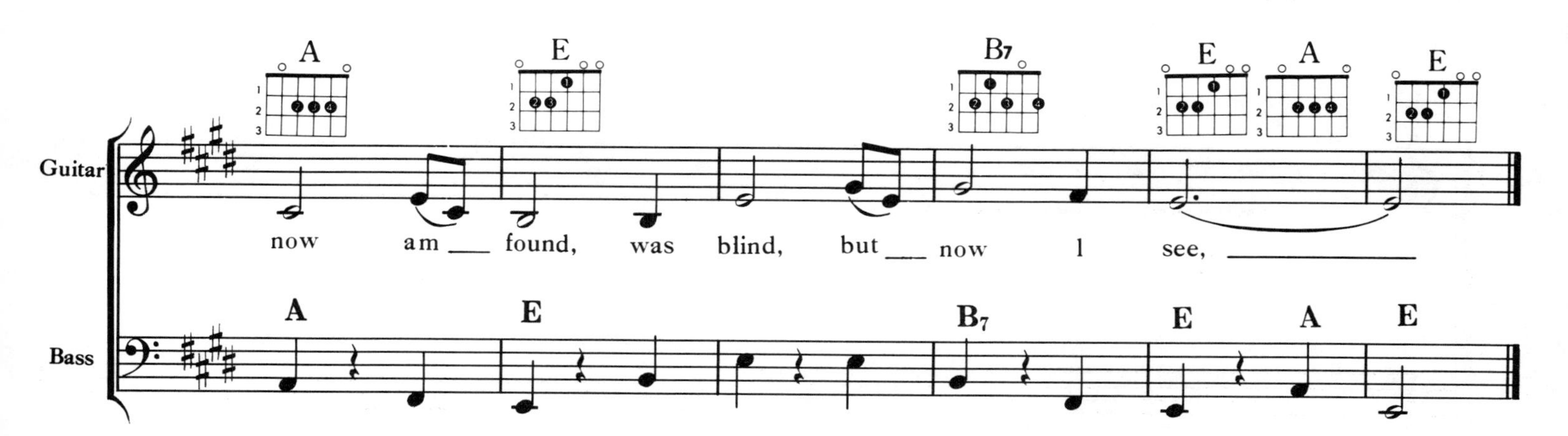

2. Twas grace that taught my heart to fear,
And grace my fear relieved
How Precious did that grace appear,
The hour I first believed

3. When we've been there ten thousand years,
Bright shining as the sun
we've no less days to sing God's praise,
Then when we first begun

ANOTHER GOSPEL PATTERN

He's Got The Whole World In His Hands

2. He's got the tiny baby in His Hands,
He's got the tiny baby in His Hands,
He's got the tiny baby in His Hands,
He's got the whole world in His hands.

3. He's got the big sky in His hands,
He's got the tiny sparrow in His hands,
He's got the tall oak trees in His hands,
He's got the whole world in His hands.

4. And He's got you'n me, brother, in His hands,
And He's got you'n me, sister, in His hands,
Oh He's got everybody in His hands,
He's got the whole world in His hands.

ANOTHER ROCK PATTERN

Boogie Bop

BLUES BALLAD STYLE

Sometimes I Feel Like A Motherless Child